Pennie Stoyles and Christine Mulvany

The A–Z of
Scientific
Discoveries

Volume 1 A–C

Smart Apple Media

Smart Apple Media
P.O. Box 3263
Mankato, MN, 56002

First published in 2009 by
MACMILLAN EDUCATION AUSTRALIA PTY LTD
15–19 Claremont Street, South Yarra, Australia 3141

Visit our web site at www.macmillan.com.au or go directly to www.macmillanlibrary.com.au

Associated companies and representatives throughout the world.

Copyright © Pennie Stoyles and Christine Mulvany 2009

Library of Congress Cataloging-in-Publication Data

Stoyles, Pennie.
  The A to Z of scientific discoveries / Pennie Stoyles and Christine Mulvany.
     p. cm.
  Includes index.
  ISBN 978-1-59920-445-1 (hardcover)
  ISBN 978-1-59920-446-8 (hardcover)
  ISBN 978-1-59920-447-5 (hardcover)
  ISBN 978-1-59920-448-2 (hardcover)
  ISBN 978-1-59920-449-9 (hardcover)
  ISBN 978-1-59920-450-5 (hardcover)
  1. Discoveries in science--Encyclopedias, Juvenile. I. Mulvany, Christine. II. Title.
  Q180.55.D57S76 2010
  503--dc22
                        2009003443

Edited by Kath Kovac
Text and cover design by Ivan Finnegan, iF Design
Page layout by Ivan Finnegan, iF Design
Photo research by Legend Images
Illustrations by Alan Laver, Shelly Communications
Solar system illustration (page 8) by Melissa Webb
Circulatory system illustration (page 26) by Jeff Lang

Printed in the United States

Acknowledgments
The author and the publisher are grateful to the following for permission to reproduce copyright
material:

Front cover photograph: Halley's Comet courtesy of James Balog/Getty Images

Photos courtesy of: Digital Vision, **5** (left); James Balog/Getty Images, **31**; Hulton Archive/
Getty Images, **22**, **30** (bottom); Keystone/Getty Images, **18** (left); Roger Viollet Collection/Getty
Images, **20** (left); Phil Walter/Getty Images, **7**; © DHuss/iStockphoto, **5** (center); © David Lewis/
iStockphoto, **18** (right); © stevecoleccs/iStockphoto, **25** (left); Library of Congress, **11** (bottom);
NASA, **16**; NASA Goddard Space Flight Center, **28**; NASA, ESA, J. Parker (Southwest Research
Institute), P. Thomas (Cornell University), L. McFadden (University of Maryland, College Park),
and M. Mutchler and Z. Levay (STScI), **9**; Photolibrary, **6**; Photolibrary/Grahame McConnell,
4; Photolibrary/John Durham/Science Photo Library, **23** (right); Photolibrary/NASA/Science
Photo Library, **17**; Photolibrary/Kent Wood, **23** (left); Photos.com, **10**; © Benis Arapovic/
Shutterstock, **24**; © Daniel Padavona/Shutterstock, **20** (right); © Principal/Shutterstock,
27; © Tyler Olson/Shutterstock, **5** (right); © Danny Smythe/Shutterstock, **25** (right); © Dave
Thompson/Shutterstock, **13**; © vladm/Shutterstock, **19**

Scientific Discoveries

Welcome to the Exciting World of Scientific Discoveries.

The A–Z of Scientific Discoveries is about the discovery and explanation of natural things. A scientific discovery can mean:

- finding or identifying something that exists in nature
- developing a theory that helps describe and explain a natural thing or event

A scientific discovery is sometimes the work of one person. Sometimes it is a series of discoveries made by many people building upon each other's ideas.

Volume 1 A–C — Scientific Discoveries

Aluminum	4
Anesthetics	6
Asteroid Belt	8
Atoms	10
Bacteria	12
Big Bang Theory	14
Black Holes	16
Blood Types	18
Buoyancy	20
Cells	22
Chlorine	24
Circulation	26
Circumference of Earth	28
Comets	30

They Said It!

"The secret to discovery is to never believe existing facts."

Bryant H. McGill, author

Aluminum

Aluminum is a silver-colored metal **element**. It is strong, very light and does not **corrode** easily.

How Aluminum Was Discovered

Aluminum is the most common metal on Earth, but it was not discovered until the early 1800s. Aluminum is never found by itself in nature. It is always combined with other elements in Earth's crust. The main source of aluminum is a **mineral** called bauxite.

English scientist Sir Humphrey Davy named aluminum in 1805. He had never actually seen it, and could not purify it, but he knew it existed. In 1825, Danish scientist Hans Christian Oersted was the first to make tiny pieces of pure aluminum.

Aluminum is extracted from bauxite, which is mined from near the surface of Earth.

Aluminum Timeline

1805	1821	1886	1950s
Sir Humphrey Davy named aluminum	Bauxite was discovered in and named after the village of Les Baux, France	Charles Hall and Paul Héroult produced pure aluminum	First aluminum drink can was made

Making Pure Aluminum

At first, purifying aluminum was very difficult and expensive. Pure aluminum was rare, and almost as precious as silver and gold. In 1886, French scientist Paul Héroult and American scientist Charles Hall used electricity to purify aluminum. Because aluminum could then be made more cheaply and easily, it began to be used in many ways.

Space shuttles, stadium seating, and wind turbines are all made from aluminum.

Aluminum in Everyday Life

Aluminum is used to make airplanes, cars, trucks, trains, building frames, and outdoor furniture. Most high-voltage power cables are made from aluminum. At home, aluminum foil is used for cooking and aluminum cans hold drinks. NASA's space shuttles are about 90 percent aluminum.

? *Did You Know?*
Today, aluminum is the most widely used metal after iron.

GLOSSARY WORDS

element	a substance made up of one type of atom
corrode	be gradually eaten away
mineral	rock that contains metals combined with other substances

Anesthetics

Anesthetics are medicines used during operations to make patients numb or unconscious, so that they don't feel pain. The word anesthetic means "without sensation."

How Anesthetics Were Discovered

Thousands of years ago, Chinese people used **acupuncture** to dull pain. Other civilizations used medicines made from various plants and often mixed them with alcohol.

English scientist Joseph Priestley discovered the first modern anesthetic, nitrous oxide (laughing gas), in 1772. In 1818, another English scientist, Michael Faraday, discovered that breathing in a gas called ether also acted as an anesthetic. In 1846, American dentist William Morton showed that he could painlessly remove a patient's tooth using ether as an anesthetic. One year later, Scottish doctor James Simpson showed that the fumes from a liquid called chloroform could help reduce the pain of childbirth.

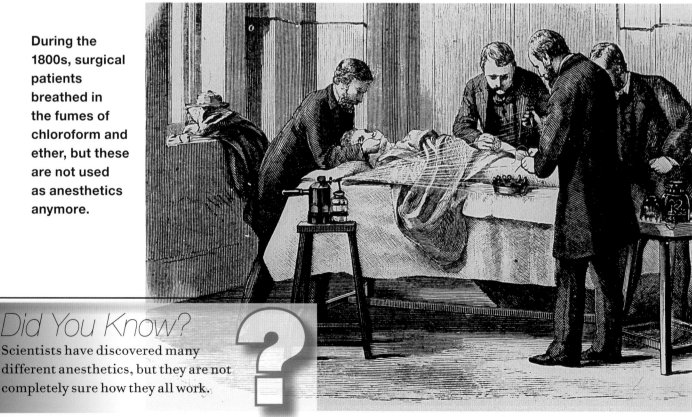

During the 1800s, surgical patients breathed in the fumes of chloroform and ether, but these are not used as anesthetics anymore.

Did You Know?
Scientists have discovered many different anesthetics, but they are not completely sure how they all work.

Anesthetics Today

When anesthetics were first discovered, people did not trust them. In the mid-1800s, England's Queen Victoria was given chloroform during childbirth. This gave people confidence in anesthetics, and they became more widely used.

Many different sorts of anesthetics are used today. Local anesthetics are usually given by injection. They numb only a small area, and the patient stays awake and alert. General anesthetics, which are used for major surgical operations, make the patient unconscious and numb all over. An epidural anesthetic is injected into the patient's spine. The patient stays awake, but the lower half of their body goes numb.

General and epidural anesthetics are given by specially trained doctors called anaesthetists. These doctors also monitor patients' breathing, heartbeat, and blood pressure during surgery.

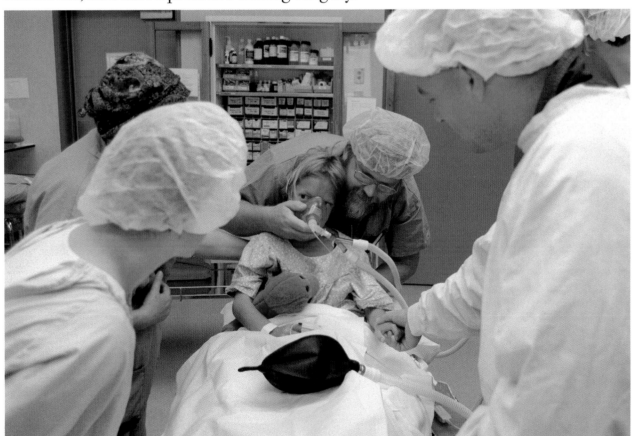

Anesthetics can be given as a gas that the patient breathes in through a mask, or as an injection into the bloodstream.

GLOSSARY WORD

acupuncture placing very fine needles into the skin to dull pain

Asteroid Belt

The main asteroid belt is a region of rocky fragments found between the orbits of Mars and Jupiter. It is about 260 million miles (419 million km) from the Sun.

The Discovery of the Asteroid Belt and Ceres

Scientists had predicted that something lay between Mars and Jupiter for a long time. In 1800, the search for these objects began. The largest objects in the asteroid belt were discovered first. Italian **astronomer** Giuseppe Piazzi discovered Ceres in 1801 and German astronomer Heinrich Olbers discovered Pallas in 1802. In 2006, Ceres was reclassified as a dwarf planet, because although it is ball-shaped and orbits the Sun, its **gravity** is not strong enough to clear the path of its orbit. This means that its orbit contains other fragments that make up the asteroid belt.

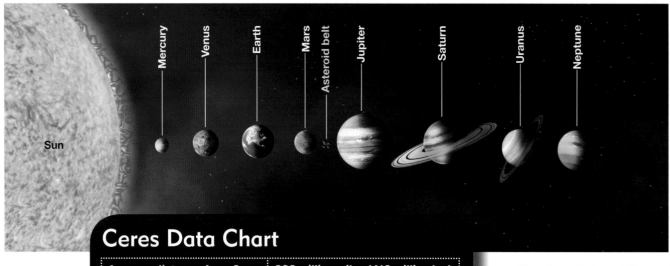

Ceres Data Chart

Average distance from Sun	260 million miles (419 million km)
Diameter at equator	590 miles (950 km)
Composition	Rocky core with an icy mantle
Moons	No
Rings	No
Mean temperature	−106°C
Time to orbit the Sun	4.6 Earth years
Rotation on axis	9 hours 4 minutes
Gravity	1/33 of the gravity of Earth

The dwarf planet Ceres is in the asteroid belt, which was discovered between Mars and Jupiter.

Discovering a New Category of Space Objects

Pallas and Ceres looked like distant stars through a telescope, but they moved too fast to be stars. In 1802, British scientist William Herschel suggested a new category, asteroids, from the Greek word *asteroeides*, which means star-like.

In 1891, astronomers mounted a camera to a telescope that tracked a point in the sky, so that the area remained in focus even though the Earth was rotating. This meant asteroids could be photographed. As technology has improved, many more asteroids have been detected. More than 200 asteroids with a diameter greater than 62 miles (100 km) have been discovered. At least 750,000 asteroids are more than 0.6 miles (1 km) in diameter, and there are millions of smaller asteroids.

The dwarf planet Ceres is the largest object in the asteroid belt.

Did You Know?

The spacecraft *Dawn Mission*, launched in 2007, is due to reach Ceres in 2015. It will make more discoveries about the asteroid belt.

GLOSSARY WORDS

astronomer scientist who studies the stars and planets
gravity the force of attraction between two objects

Atoms

Everything in the universe is made up of extremely tiny particles called atoms.

Ancient Ideas About Atoms

The idea that all things are made up of tiny particles began in ancient Greece. In about 500 BC, Greek scholars Leucippus and Democritus believed that all matter was made from tiny hard particles separated by empty space. Roman poet Lucretius wrote about atoms in 50 BC. His poem stated that atoms could not be destroyed and that they lasted forever.

John Dalton

In 1808, English scientist John Dalton wrote that all matter is made of atoms, which are unchangeable. He also said that different atoms can combine to form compounds, and that chemical reactions occur when atoms are rearranged. Dalton's ideas were widely accepted by scientists at the time. Later, scientists did discover how to change atoms.

Did You Know?

About 115 different types of atoms have been discovered. Only 91 occur naturally on Earth; the rest have been made in laboratories.

Scientist John Dalton used these symbols for different atoms. Today, we use letters such as **S** for sulfur and **N** for nitrogen to represent atoms.

Inside an Atom

In 1897, British physicist Joseph Thomson discovered that atoms contained even smaller particles called **electrons**. In the 1900s, New Zealand scientist Ernest Rutherford and Danish scientist Niels Bohr discovered that electrons spin around the atom's center, called the nucleus. Rutherford also named particles found within the nucleus, calling them **protons**. In 1934, English physicist James Chadwick discovered that the nucleus contains another type of particle, called **neutrons**.

We now know that each type of atom has a different number of protons, neutrons, and electrons. Each atom is given an atomic number, which is the number of protons it contains. Hydrogen is number 1, and oxygen is number 8.

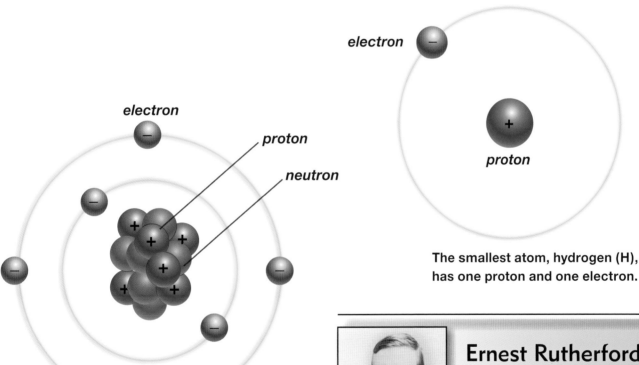

The smallest atom, hydrogen (H), has one proton and one electron.

Carbon (C) has six protons, six neutrons, and six electrons.

Ernest Rutherford (1871–1937)

Element number 104, rutherfordium, is named after Rutherford. Ernest Rutherford won the Nobel Prize for Chemistry in 1908 for his discoveries about atoms.

GLOSSARY WORDS

electrons	particles that spin around the nucleus of an atom
protons	particles found in the nucleus of all atoms
neutrons	particles found in the nucleus of all atoms except hydrogen

Bacteria

Bacteria are **microscopic** single-celled living things. They are found almost everywhere on Earth.

How Bacteria Were Discovered

In 1676, Dutch scientist Anton van Leeuwenhoek observed the first bacteria. He examined the material from his mouth using a microscope that made objects appear 300 times bigger than their true size. The term "bacteria" was not introduced until 1838. In 1884, Danish bacteriologist Hans Christian Gram developed a stain that made it easier to see the structure of the bacterial cell wall. As microscopes improved, even more detail could be seen. The development of the electron microscope in the 1930s meant that bacteria could be magnified 200,000 times.

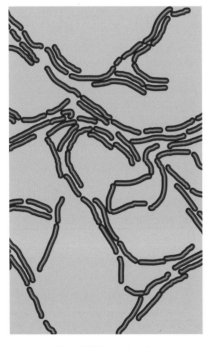
bacilli bacteria

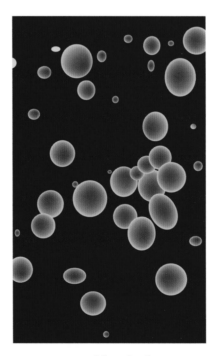
cocci bacteria

spirilla bacteria

Anton van Leeuwenhoek grouped bacteria by shape; bacilli bacteria are rod-shaped (left), cocci bacteria are ball-shaped (middle), and spirilla bacteria are spiral-shaped (right).

Did You Know?

Listerine® mouthwash is named after English surgeon, Joseph Lister. In 1867, Lister discovered that bacterial infections were reduced by cleaning tools, hands, and wounds with carbolic acid during surgery.

Bacteria in Everyday Life

In the mid-1800s, scientists discovered that some bacteria were harmful and caused disease. Tetanus, pneumonia, food poisoning, and leprosy are all caused by bacteria.

Other bacteria are very useful. Human intestines contain more than 300 types of bacteria to help them function. Medical, mining, and food industries all use bacteria. Some bacteria break down waste and play an important role in sewerage treatment. Others help plants to grow by converting nitrogen in the air to a form that can be taken up by the roots.

Bacteria and the Evolution of Life

Cyanobacteria, which usually live in water, can produce their own food and give off oxygen. Fossils of cyanobacteria that date back 3.5 billion years have been found. Scientists believe that these bacteria helped create an **atmosphere** with levels of oxygen that made it possible for other life forms to develop.

Bacteria are used to make artificial sweeteners that are used in many diet products, including soft drinks.

GLOSSARY WORDS

microscopic   too small to be seen without a microscope
atmosphere   layer of gases surrounding a planet

Big Bang Theory

The Big Bang theory states that the universe began expanding after a huge explosion about 13.7 **billion** years ago.

How the Big Bang Theory Was Discovered

In 1931, Belgian mathematician George Lemaitre published the idea now known as the Big Bang theory. Like many discoveries, this theory was built on previous ideas.

In 1922, Russian mathematician Alexander Friedman devised an equation that showed the universe could expand. By 1927, Lemaitre had discovered that **galaxies** were moving away from each other. Two years later, American astronomer Edwin Hubble confirmed that the universe was expanding. Lemaitre then thought that if the universe is expanding now, in the past it must have started with an explosion at a single point in time.

Big Bang

The universe might have looked like this just after the Big Bang. Gases cooled and clumped together to form galaxies.

Universe Timeline

13.7 billion years ago	**5** billion years ago	**4.5** billion years ago	**3.8** billion years ago
The Big Bang causes galaxies to begin to form	The Sun forms	Earth forms	First life appears on Earth

Finding Support for the Big Bang Theory

Since 1931, other scientists have found evidence to support the Big Bang theory. In 1948, Russian physicist George Gamow predicted that if there was a giant explosion, then an afterglow known as cosmic background radiation should be detected. It was discovered in 1964.

In 1989, the National Aeronautics and Space Administration (NASA) launched a satellite called the Cosmic Background Explorer to measure cosmic background radiation. In 2001, NASA launched the Wilkinson Microwave Anisotropy Probe (WMAP) to measure cosmic background radiation with even (greater accuracy. From data collected by WMAP, scientists believe that the universe began about 13.7 billion years ago.

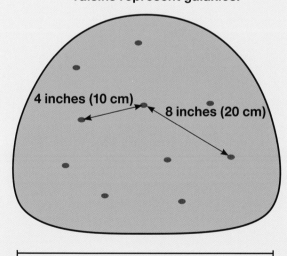

2 inches (5 cm)
4 inches (10 cm)
8 inches (20 cm)

The universe can be seen as a ball of dough. The raisins represent galaxies.

4 inches (10 cm)
8 inches (20 cm)
16 inches (40 cm)

As the dough expands, the raisins stay the same size but the distance between them increases.

George Lemaitre (1894–1966)

George Lemaitre was a Belgian mathematician, physics professor, astronomer, and Catholic priest. He is known as "the father of the Big Bang Theory."

GLOSSARY WORDS

billion   one thousand million
galaxies   huge collections of stars, dust, and gas held together by gravity

Black Holes

A black hole is a tiny region of space that has an enormous mass. Not even light can escape a black hole's immense **gravitational pull**.

Forming the Idea of Black Holes

The idea of a black hole developed as scientists built upon previous discoveries. In 1687, Isaac Newton developed the idea of gravity: that objects with mass attract one another. In the late 1700s, English scientist John Michell and French astronomer Pierre-Simon Laplace both described the possibility of a "dark star" with such a strong gravitational pull that light could not escape.

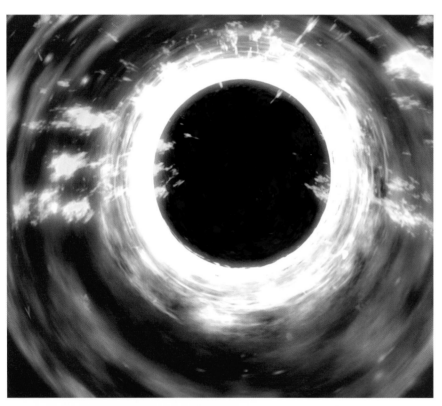

A black hole has such a massive gravitational pull that it pulls everything towards itself, including light.

Albert Einstein further developed the idea of gravity during the early 1900s. In 1916, German astronomer Karl Schwarzschild worked out how close, in theory, you could get to the center of a "dark star" before being trapped by its gravitational pull. In 1967, American physicist John Wheeler introduced the term "black hole."

John Archibald Wheeler (1911–2008)

John Wheeler was an American professor of physics. He is well-known for his part in the production of the atomic bomb.

Discovering a Black Hole

As black holes trap light, they cannot actually be seen. They are detected by their effect on nearby objects, such as gas and dust, which swirl around the black hole. The swirling matter heats up and **emits** X rays. In 1972, the UHURU X ray satellite discovered the first black hole. The Chandra X ray Observatory and the XMM-Newton X ray satellite have since discovered many other black holes.

The UHURU X ray satellite can detect X rays emitted by matter swirling around a black hole.

Types of Black Holes

A dying massive star produces a stellar black hole. The mass left after the star's explosion is at least three times bigger than our Sun, and it can be compressed into a very small region. A super massive black hole is found at the center of galaxies. It has a mass around 1 million to 1 billion times bigger than the Sun.

Did You Know?

The closest stellar black hole to Earth is 1,600 **light years** away. The nearest super massive black hole is at the center of the Milky Way Galaxy, 28,000 light years away.

GLOSSARY WORDS

gravitational pull	attraction that an object has for another object due to gravity
emits	sends outwards: for example, the Sun emits light and heat
light year	the distance traveled by light in one year: about 6.2 trillion miles (10 trillion km)

Blood Types

Blood is grouped into different types based on the **antigens** found on the surface of red blood cells.

Why Blood Types Are Important

In the past, doctors tried taking blood from one person and giving it to a patient. As nobody knew about blood types, the patient often received the incorrect type of blood. When this happened, the body's defense system started attacking itself and the patient died. In 1907, the first successful blood **transfusion** was made using knowledge of blood types.

How Blood Types Were Discovered

Blood types were discovered in 1900 by American scientist Karl Landsteiner. He noticed that blood from different people sometimes formed clumps. He classified each type according to how it reacted when mixed with other blood samples. Blood types were first suggested to be **inherited** in 1907 by American **hematologist** Reuben Ottenberg.

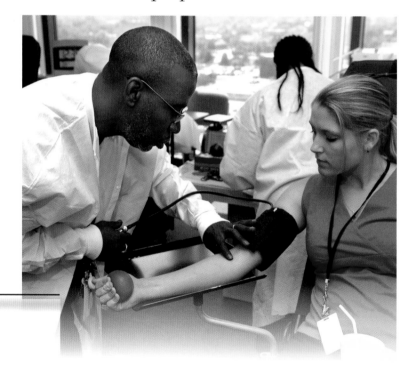

Donating blood can help people survive blood losses from accidents or during surgery.

Karl Landsteiner (1868–1943)

Karl Landsteiner was born in Austria, and later became an American citizen. Apart from his discovery of blood types, he also studied how the body fights diseases. In 1930, he was awarded the Nobel Prize for Physiology.

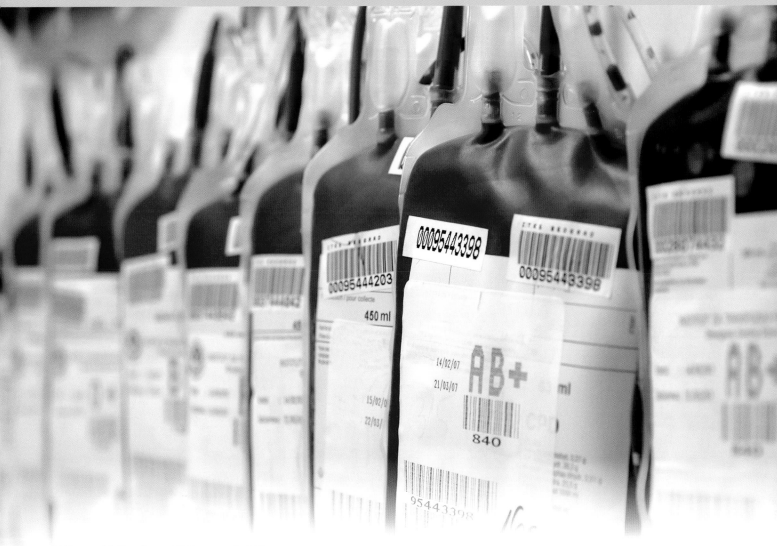

The Main Blood Types

Of the 30 blood group systems that exist, the ABO blood group system is the most common. It is based on the presence of antigens A and B. The four basic groups are A (contains only the A antigen), B (contains only the B antigen), AB (contains both), and O (contains neither).

The second most common grouping is the Rhesus blood group system. These groups are positive (if the Rhesus antigen is present) and negative (if it is absent).

Blood is stored in tough plastic bags that are clearly labeled with the blood type.

Did You Know?

The most common blood groups in the world are O positive and A positive. The rarest is AB negative. Four out of every five people in the world are positive for the Rhesus antigen.

GLOSSARY WORDS

antigens	substances that trigger the body's defense system
transfusion	the process of transferring fluid
inherited	passed from parents to their children
hematologist	a doctor specializing in blood diseases

Buoyancy

Buoyancy explains why some things sink and other things float.

How Buoyancy Was Discovered

Buoyancy is explained by the Archimedes principle. It was discovered by the Ancient Greek scientist Archimedes more than 2,200 years ago. Archimedes supposedly discovered the idea when he realized that the water level changed when he sat in the bath.

Buoyancy in Everyday Life

Buoyancy is considered when designers plan huge container ships and submarines. Buoyancy is at work when partygoers fill balloons with helium, and when children learn to swim using a kickboard and floaties.

Children learning to swim often use flotation aids that are lighter than the water they push aside.

Archimedes of Syracuse (c. 287–212 BC)

Archimedes was a mathematician, engineer, and scientist. One of his great discoveries was finding the value of **pi**. He also invented many devices such as the Archimedes screw (a device for raising water), the catapult, and the compound pulley system.

Buoyancy and Fluid

When an object is placed in a **fluid** (such as water or air), it pushes aside the fluid. This **displaced** fluid pushes back at the object, effectively upwards. Archimedes' principle states that this upward push is equal to the weight of the displaced fluid. The amount of fluid displaced can be found by measuring the difference in fluid levels after an object is put into a container.

Mass is measured in ounces, and weight is measured in **newtons**. On Earth, the weight of something is its mass multiplied by the force of gravity. One pound weighs about 5 newtons, and 1 ounce weighs about 0.28 newtons.

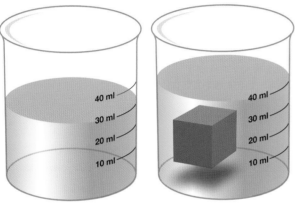

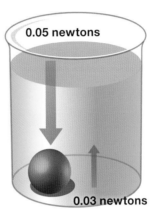

0.05 newtons

0.03 newtons

2. If a ball of modeling putty weighing 0.05 newtons displaced 3 milliliters of water, its buoyancy force would be 0.03 newtons. The weight is greater than the buoyancy force so the putty would sink.

1. The block in the second beaker has displaced 10 milliliters of water, causing the water level to rise. One milliliter of water has a mass of 0.03 ounces, so if the block displaces 10 milliliters of water it has a mass of 0.03 ounces and a weight of 0.1 newtons. The buoyancy force is the same as the weight of the fluid, so the block has a buoyancy force of 0.1 newtons.

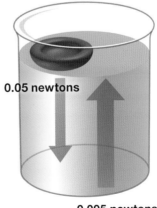

0.05 newtons

0.095 newtons

3. If the same piece of putty was remodeled into a boat shape, then air would displace some of the water and the putty's buoyancy force would be greater. If the putty displaced 9.5 milliliters of water, its buoyancy force would be equal to 0.095 newtons. This is greater than the weight of the putty, so the putty would float.

GLOSSARY WORDS

pi	a number used to show the ratio of a circle's circumference to its diameter
fluid	liquid or gas
displaced	pushed aside
newtons	a unit of force named after Sir Isaac Newton

Cc Cells

Every living thing is made up of cells. Some living things are a single cell, but most are made of millions of different cells.

How Cells Were Discovered

Most cells are too small to be seen with the naked eye. Therefore, they were not discovered until after microscopes were invented. In 1665, English scientist Robert Hooke examined a thin slice of cork under a microscope. He saw what looked like a lot of tiny boxes with walls, and called the shapes *cells*, which means little boxes.

Looking Inside Cells

As microscopes improved, more cell types were discovered. In 1831 Scottish **botanist** Robert Brown discovered that all plant cells contained an **organelle**, which he named the nucleus. He thought, correctly, that the nucleus had something to do with cell reproduction. Cells reproduce by dividing in half to produce two identical cells.

Robert Hooke used a microscope to discover cells.

Robert Hooke (1635–1703)

Robert Hooke studied many different areas of science and mathematics. He discovered cells and studied astronomy, and is famous for working out the mathematics of coiled springs. He also helped to design several famous buildings in London.

How Cells Work

Different types of cells do different things; brain cells help us think, muscle cells help us move, and red blood cells carry oxygen around our bodies. However, all cells share some common features, whether they come from plants, animals, or any other living thing. They are all like tiny bags of jelly. The "jelly" is called cytoplasm (say SY-toe-pla-zum), and the "bag" is the cell **membrane** that surrounds the cytoplasm. The cytoplasm contains many types of organelles with different functions.

Animal cells (left) and plant cells (above) both have cell membranes, but plant cells have defined cell walls.

Did You Know?
A single drop of blood contains millions of blood cells.

GLOSSARY WORDS

botanist — scientist who studies plants
organelle — part of a cell that does a particular job
membrane — very thin skin

Chlorine

Chlorine is the 17th most common element in the universe. It is never found by itself in nature and is always combined with other **elements**.

How Chlorine Was Discovered

Pure chlorine was discovered by Swedish chemist Carl Scheele in 1774. While experimenting with hydrochloric acid, he noticed that a gas with a suffocating smell was produced. The gas killed a nearby bee, and bleached the color out of flowers and leaves.

In 1810, English scientist Sir Humphry Davies showed that chlorine was an element. He named it after the Greek word *chloros*, which means green. The chemical symbol for chlorine is Cl. It is element 17 because its nucleus contains 17 protons.

Chlorine is added to public swimming pools to kill germs in the water.

Chlorine and Salt

Pure chlorine is made from salt water. Common table salt contains chlorine combined with another element, sodium. Salt has been an important part of our history for thousands of years. It is used to preserve and flavor food. We must have a certain amount of salt in our diets to stay healthy, but eating too much can be unhealthy.

Chlorine in Everyday Life

Chlorine is used to manufacture lots of useful products, including many types of plastic. Chlorine is also used to whiten paper, and chlorine-based bleach is used for cleaning and whitening clothes.

The chemical name for table salt is sodium chloride, and its chemical symbol is NaCl.

Chlorine is used in the manufacture of polyvinyl chloride (PVC), a type of waterproof plastic used to make raincoats and water pipes and hoses.

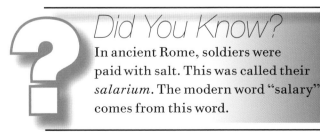

Did You Know?

In ancient Rome, soldiers were paid with salt. This was called their *salarium*. The modern word "salary" comes from this word.

GLOSSARY WORD

elements   substances made of only one type of atom

Circulation

Blood **circulation** is the movement of blood around the body. Blood is pumped through the blood vessels by the heart.

How Circulation Was Discovered

In 1628, an English doctor, William Harvey, discovered how circulation works. He researched the workings of the body by studying animals and dead bodies. Harvey described the heart as a pump, and noticed that the blood flows around the body in one direction. He worked out that the amount of blood pumped in one hour was three times the body weight of a person. This led him to the idea that the same blood was circulating around the body.

heart

The heart pumps blood around the body.

William Harvey (1578–1657)

William Harvey was the Court Physician (official doctor) to both King James I and King Charles I of England. He discovered how blood circulates through the body.

More Proof of Blood Circulation

Before Harvey's discovery, people thought that blood was made in the liver and traveled once through the veins to the rest of the body, before it was used up. When Harvey described his theory of blood circulation, it took a while for people to believe it.

In 1661, Italian doctor Marcello Malpighi discovered the tiny capillaries that join together the veins and arteries. This provided further proof that the blood flowed in a circular motion. Malpighi also discovered red blood cells and nerves, as well as how air gets from the lungs into the blood.

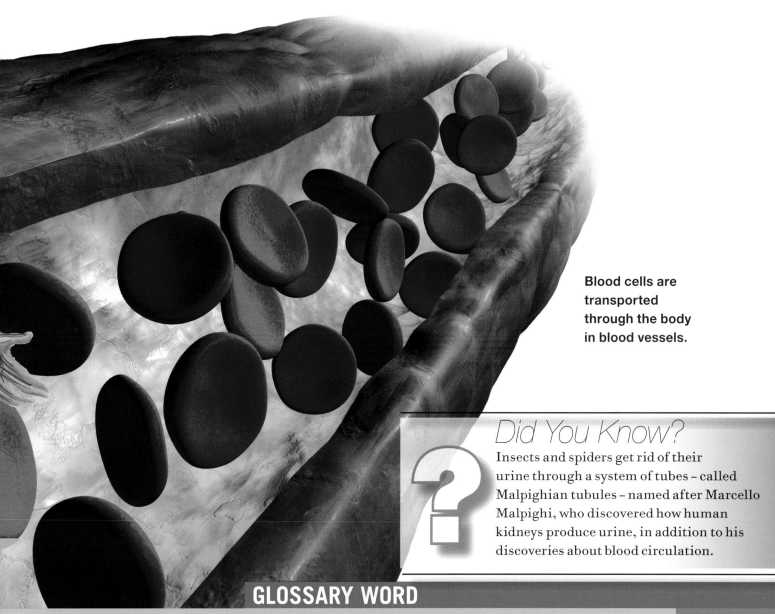

Blood cells are transported through the body in blood vessels.

Did You Know?

Insects and spiders get rid of their urine through a system of tubes – called Malpighian tubules – named after Marcello Malpighi, who discovered how human kidneys produce urine, in addition to his discoveries about blood circulation.

GLOSSARY WORD
circulation   going in a circle

Circumference of Earth

The circumference of Earth is the distance around its widest part. It is 24,901 miles (40,075 km).

How the Circumference of Earth Was Discovered

The Ancient Greeks knew that Earth was a **sphere**. They noticed that during an **eclipse**, the shadow that Earth made on the Moon was always circle-shaped, which could only be made by a sphere. More than 2,000 years ago, Greek librarian, Eratosthenes, discovered how to measure the circumference of Earth using mathematical equations.

People have known that Earth is a sphere for thousands of years.

Did You Know?

Earth is not a perfect sphere; it is a bit wider at the equator. The distance around the equator is 24,901 miles (40,075 km), but around the poles it is 24,859 miles (40,008 km).

Calculating the Circumference of Earth

Imagine Earth as an orange cut in half, allowing you to see the segments that meet in the center. The central angle is the angle of each segment at the center. If you know the central angle, then you know how many segments will fit in the circle. Since there are 360 degrees in a circle, if the central angle is 60 degrees, you know that six segments can fit, because 6 x 60 = 360.

Eratosthenes discovered how to calculate the central angle between two towns using shadow sticks. He found the central angle between the towns of Alexandria and Syene, which were about 522 miles (840 km) apart, was 7 degrees – about 1/50th of 360 degrees. He calculated that because Earth was a sphere, 50 "Alexandria to Syene" segments would fit around the circumference of Earth. He came up with a value of 50 segments x 522 miles (840 km) = 26,097 miles (42,000 km), which is very close to the actual value we know today.

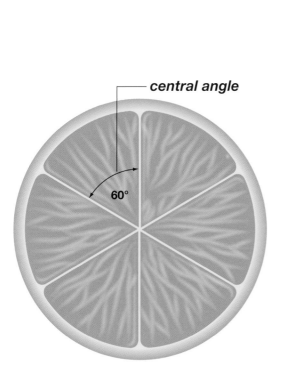

In this orange, the central angle is 60 degrees. Six segments will fit in the 360 degree circle.

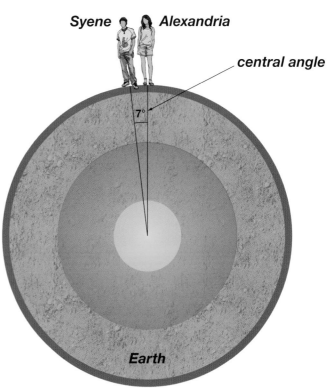

The central angle between Syene and Alexandria is 7 degrees. Fifty 7-degree segments will fit in the 360 degree circle of Earth.

GLOSSARY WORDS

sphere   ball-shaped
eclipse   to block the light coming from one object with another object

29

Comets

Comets are irregular-shaped objects made from dust and ice. They travel in unusual orbits that take them close to the Sun and back out past Neptune.

How Comets Were Discovered

People have observed comets since ancient times, though they often misunderstood them as warning signs from the gods. Comets began to be tracked after the invention of the telescope in the 1600s. By the start of the 1700s, scientists realized that some comets might be the same ones reappearing. In the mid 1980s and early 2000s, spacecraft sent to collect data from comets revealed their composition.

More than 3,500 comets have now been been named and had their orbits calculated. About 200 comets, thought to originate from the Kuiper belt, have an **orbital period** of less than 200 years. The remainder are thought to originate in the **Oort cloud**.

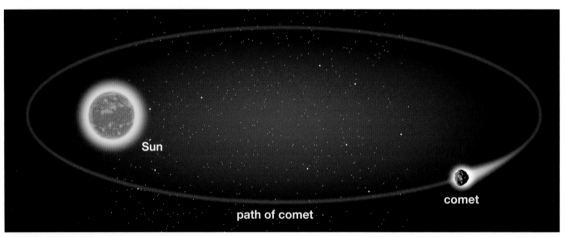

Sun

path of comet

comet

A comet can usually make about 500 irregular orbits past the Sun before it loses its ice and gas and becomes just a rocky object.

Edmund Halley (1656–1742)

Edmund Halley was an English astronomer who recognized that a comet described in 1531, 1607, and 1682 was the same one reappearing. He accurately predicted that the comet would return in 1758. It was named Comet Halley in his honor.

A Comet's Characteristic Tail

When a comet comes close to the Sun, some of its ice changes into gas, and solar winds create a huge gas tail on the comet. The tail always points away from the Sun. It is behind the **comet's nucleus** as it travels toward the Sun, and in front as it travels away.

Naming Comets

Comets were originally named after the instrument or person that made the discovery. In 1994, an official naming system was introduced that gives every comet an individual number and letter combination. This provides information about when it was discovered and the order of its discovery.

Comet Halley is officially known as 1P/1682 Q1. The 1 shows it was the first comet discovered; P shows it is a periodic comet; and 1682 was the year it was discovered. Q indicates that it was seen in the first half of September (A is given to the first half of January and each half month is given the next letter in the alphabet.) The final 1 indicates that it was the first comet seen in that half month.

Comet Halley can be seen with the naked eye when it passes Earth every 76–79 years. It is due to return in 2061.

Did You Know?

The word comet comes from the Greek *aster kometes*, which means long-haired star and refers to the comet's tail.

GLOSSARY WORDS

orbital period   time taken to orbit the Sun
Oort cloud   a region of icy bodies 50–100 times further away than the distance from Earth to the Sun
comet's nucleus   the solid section of the comet

Index

Page references in bold indicate that there is a full entry for that discovery.

A

ABO blood group
   system 19
aluminum **4–5**
anesthetics **6–7**
Archimedes of
   Syracuse 20
Archimedes
   principle 20, 21
asteroid belt **8–9**
atoms **10–11**

B

bacteria **12–13**
Big Bang theory
   14–15
black holes **16–17**
blood types **18–19**
Bohr, Neils 11
Brown, Robert 22
buoyancy **20–21**

C

cells **22–23**
Ceres 8, 9
Chadwick, James 11
chlorine **24–25**
chloroform 6, 7
circulation **26–27**
circumference,
   Earth **28–29**
Comet Halley 31
comets **30–31**
cyanobacteria 13

D

Dalton, John 10
Davies, Sir
   Humphry 4, 24
Democritus 10

E

Einstein, Albert 16
electron 11
Eratosthenes 28, 29
ether 6, 7

F

Faraday, Michael 6
Friedman,
   Alexander 14

G

Gamow, George 15
Gram, Hans
   Christian 12

H

Hall, Charles 4, 5
Halley, Edmund 30
Harvey, William 26,
   27
Héroult, Paul 5
Herschel, William 9
Hooke, Robert 22
Hubble, Edwin 14

K

Kuiper belt 30

L

Landsteiner, Karl 18
Laplace,
   Pierre-Simon 16
Lemaitre,
   George 14, 15

M

Malpighi,
   Marcello 27
Michell, John 16
microscope 12, 22
Morton, William 6

N

neutron 11
Newton, Isaac 16
newtons 21
nitrous oxide 6

O

Oersted, Hans
   Christian 4
Olbers, Heinrich 8
Oort cloud 30, 31
Ottenberg,
   Reuben 18

P

Piazzi, Giuseppe 8
Priestley, Joseph 6
proton 11, 24

R

Rhesus antigen 19
Rutherford,
   Ernest 11

S

salt 25
Scheele, Carl 24
Schwarzchild,
   Karl 16
Simpson, James 6

T

Thomson, Joseph 11
transfusion 18, 19

V

van Leeuwenhoek,
   Anton 12

W

Wheeler, John 16